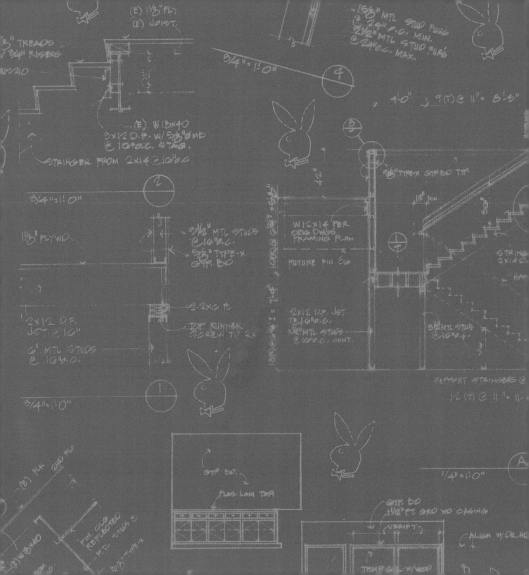

Cedco Publishing
100 Pelican Way
San Rafael, California 94901
www.cedco.com

Edited by Vanessa Brown
Cover and book design by Teena Gores

ISBN 0-7683-2520-X

Printed in China

3 5 7 9 10 8 6 4 2

MANTRACK

PLAYBOY'S
BLUEPRINTS

FOR BETTER
LIVING

Playboy made its reputation on men's fantasies. The magazine featured the most beautiful women, the fastest cars, the coolest stuff. (Oh, yes—we ran articles, too.) At the same time, *Playboy* intended to serve as a man's guide. We wanted to provide useful real information, whether it was about oral sex or trouser cuff length. We covered the waterfront. We discoursed on fashion, cooking, travel, etiquette, electronics. Mantrack, a feature that started in December 1997, was aimed at both sides of our readers' brains: the libidinal fantasy life and the more mundane proprietary urges ("I want to do that. I want that in my home"). We ran drop-dead gorgeous pictures—and we ran blueprints. The idea? To reduce information to its absolute essence. To provide a simple schematic for what might otherwise be a daunting task. We wanted readers who felt good about themselves, who could impress their girlfriends and startle their friends. Build a fire? Sew a button? Flip food? Do a roundhouse kick? We showed you how. Nurtured by Associate Managing Editor John Rezek, the blueprints were one of the most popular innovations in Mantrack and continue to be so. They are drawn by Bill Benway and stand apart as a unique mix of art and instruction.

CONTENTS

> "IF YOU LOOK GOOD
> AND DRESS WELL,
> YOU DON'T NEED
> A PURPOSE IN LIFE."
>
> — Robert Pante

DRESSING

&

IMPRESSING

TAKE A BOW

A man should know how to tie a bow tie. It needn't be perfect — in fact, perfection gives away a pre-tied knot. Use the blueprint at right (maneuver number five is crucial). You get extra points for not needing a mirror. The best part comes later, when you untie your work and hang very cool.

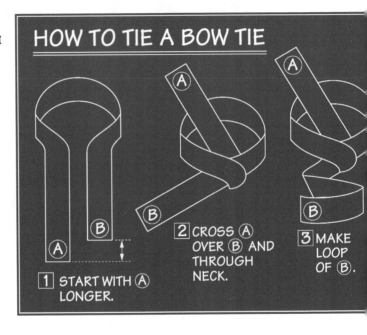

HOW TO TIE A BOW TIE

1 START WITH Ⓐ LONGER.

2 CROSS Ⓐ OVER Ⓑ AND THROUGH NECK.

3 MAKE LOOP OF Ⓑ.

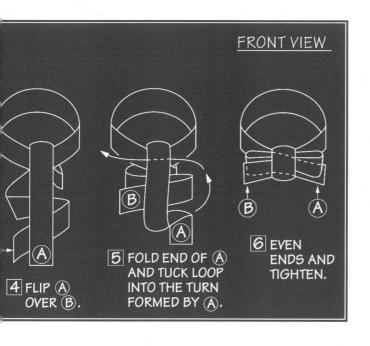

FRONT VIEW

4 FLIP Ⓐ OVER Ⓑ.

5 FOLD END OF Ⓐ AND TUCK LOOP INTO THE TURN FORMED BY Ⓐ.

6 EVEN ENDS AND TIGHTEN.

BEST FOOT FORWARD

Check your shoes for loose seams or tears. If the leather is pliable, any shoe repair shop can mend the uppers to like-new condition. Inspect for worn bottoms. Good soles will provide maximum support and keep moisture out. You can also add protective soles to your

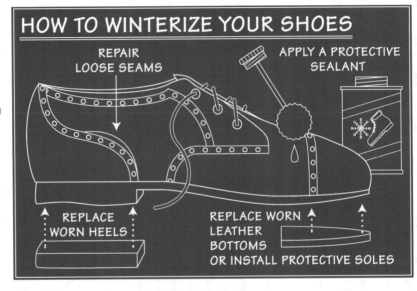

HOW TO WINTERIZE YOUR SHOES

REPAIR LOOSE SEAMS

APPLY A PROTECTIVE SEALANT

REPLACE WORN HEELS

REPLACE WORN LEATHER BOTTOMS OR INSTALL PROTECTIVE SOLES

leather-soled shoes, which increase traction, reduce the number of times you have to replace your soles and shield leather bottoms from wet conditions. Next, your shoes should be cleaned with a non-alkaline soap to remove dirt and reconditioned to restore the lubricants that keep leather supple. And whether your shoes are old or new, always apply a protectant, such as mink oil, at least once a month to guard against wet weather and salt.

Michael Felton, master head barber of The Art of Shaving in Manhattan, has some tips on getting your goatee to behave. First, it needs to be cleaned every day, but don't wash it with soap. Treat it like the hair on your head, and use the same sort of mild shampoo and conditioner you use on top. Trim it at least once a week, following the blueprint below. If you narrow the goatee while trimming, you have to shave the exposed portion of your face. Since you may have to go over that area a few times, use a preshave oil and then shaving cream when you work with the razor. When you shave the rest of your face, finish with an aftershave gel that has a moisturizer. It can be rubbed through your beard and will keep the skin beneath it healthy. Don't worry, these products will evaporate and shouldn't glop up your beard.

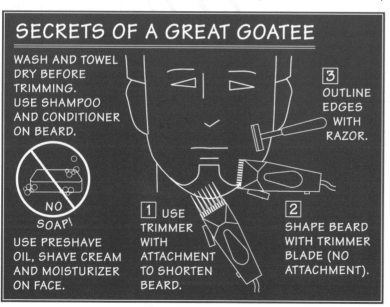

SECRETS OF A GREAT GOATEE

WASH AND TOWEL DRY BEFORE TRIMMING. USE SHAMPOO AND CONDITIONER ON BEARD.

NO SOAP!

USE PRESHAVE OIL, SHAVE CREAM AND MOISTURIZER ON FACE.

[1] USE TRIMMER WITH ATTACHMENT TO SHORTEN BEARD.

[2] SHAPE BEARD WITH TRIMMER BLADE (NO ATTACHMENT).

[3] OUTLINE EDGES WITH RAZOR.

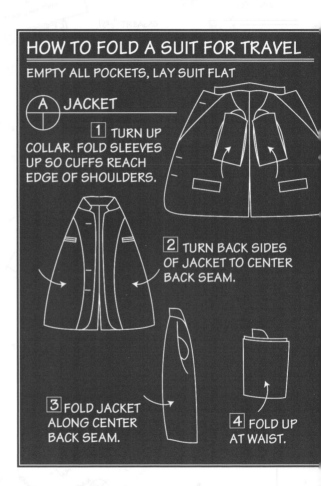

HOW TO FOLD A SUIT FOR TRAVEL

EMPTY ALL POCKETS, LAY SUIT FLAT

(A) JACKET

1 TURN UP COLLAR. FOLD SLEEVES UP SO CUFFS REACH EDGE OF SHOULDERS.

2 TURN BACK SIDES OF JACKET TO CENTER BACK SEAM.

3 FOLD JACKET ALONG CENTER BACK SEAM.

4 FOLD UP AT WAIST.

Packing It In

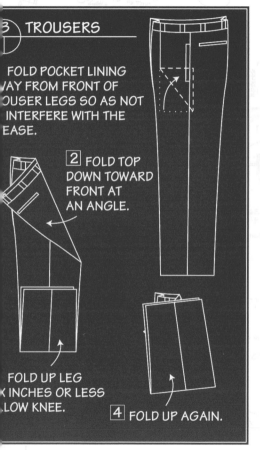

3 TROUSERS

FOLD POCKET LINING
AY FROM FRONT OF
OUSER LEGS SO AS NOT
INTERFERE WITH THE
EASE.

2 FOLD TOP
DOWN TOWARD
FRONT AT
AN ANGLE.

FOLD UP LEG
INCHES OR LESS
LOW KNEE.

4 FOLD UP AGAIN.

The folding suit bag hasn't solved all of modern man's travel problems. It doesn't always fit in an overhead compartment, and unless you're in first class, airline personnel tend to balk at hanging them up. If airlines follow through on their threats to restrict passengers to one carry-on bag, you'll need to learn the lost art of folding a suit. Our source is Stanley Ager, the ur-butler whose *Ager's Way to Easy Elegance* is a recherché hoot. We tried the method diagrammed at left on two recent trips, and our suit survived beautifully. Let your suit rest on a hanger for a few hours before you need to put it on. Finally, hang it in the bathroom when you take a shower to relax any wrinkles that haven't disappeared already.

Button Up

They come off at the worst times—you've committed to wearing a certain suit with a certain shirt, which now has a button missing. Postmodern man cannot rely on anyone to fix this problem for him. Learn the skill described at right and finally set yourself free.

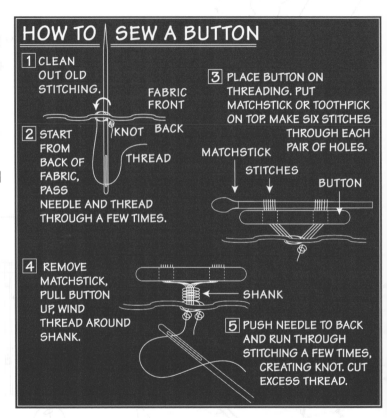

HOW TO SEW A BUTTON

1 CLEAN OUT OLD STITCHING.

FABRIC FRONT

BACK

KNOT

2 START FROM BACK OF FABRIC, PASS NEEDLE AND THREAD THROUGH A FEW TIMES.

THREAD

3 PLACE BUTTON ON THREADING. PUT MATCHSTICK OR TOOTHPICK ON TOP. MAKE SIX STITCHES THROUGH EACH PAIR OF HOLES.

MATCHSTICK

STITCHES

BUTTON

4 REMOVE MATCHSTICK, PULL BUTTON UP, WIND THREAD AROUND SHANK.

SHANK

5 PUSH NEEDLE TO BACK AND RUN THROUGH STITCHING A FEW TIMES, CREATING KNOT. CUT EXCESS THREAD.

UNSTICK LIPSTICK

Lipstick stains—on the shirt collar or on an intimate piece of clothing—are more fun to get on than off. And while some men like to wear them as a badge of honor, the shade may not go with the color scheme of your tie. Use this blueprint to erase the traces she left. When you use a nonflammable stain remover, work from the opposite side of the fabric from the stain. After a few times, you'll conclude that it's a lot easier to remove lipstick from skin than it is from clothing. Behave accordingly.

HOW TO REMOVE A LIPSTICK STAIN

1 TRY TO REMOVE THE STAIN WITH A NONFLAMMABLE STAIN REMOVER.

APPLY REMOVER TO THE FABRIC FROM THE BACK OF THE STAIN.

PUT PAPER TOWELS OR RAGS ON THE UNDERSIDE OF THE FABRIC YOU'RE WORKING ON.

2 IF THE STAIN REMAINS, USE A PREWASH STAIN REMOVER AND RINSE.

3 IF THAT DOESN'T WORK, RUB THE AREA WITH LIQUID DETERGENT AND THEN WASH IN WARM WATER.

> "IF SEX IS SUCH A NATURAL PHENOMENON, HOW COME THERE ARE SO MANY BOOKS ON HOW TO DO IT?"
>
> — Bette Midler

GIVING

RECEIVING

GET FIRED UP

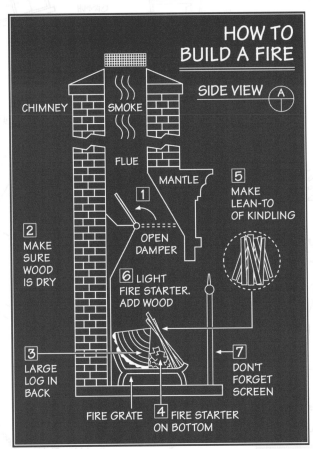

HOW TO BUILD A FIRE

SIDE VIEW Ⓐ

CHIMNEY

SMOKE

FLUE

MANTLE

1 OPEN DAMPER

2 MAKE SURE WOOD IS DRY

3 LARGE LOG IN BACK

FIRE GRATE

4 FIRE STARTER ON BOTTOM

5 MAKE LEAN-TO OF KINDLING

6 LIGHT FIRE STARTER. ADD WOOD

7 DON'T FORGET SCREEN

There's no more certain way to botch a romantic evening than to fill the condo with woodsmoke. Here's the right way to light her fire. First, make sure the damper is open. If the smoke from a match doesn't rise up the chimney, the damper is closed. Next, make sure the wood is dry. (Dry hardwood logs will make a ringing sound when knocked together.) Lay a large log at the back of the grate. Place a handful of tinder in front of that log (try birch bark or pitch-saturated fatwood sticks). Place finger-thick pieces of kindling over the fire starter, resting them against the log like a small lean-to. Light the fire starter. Allow it to ignite the kindling, then gradually add bigger pieces of wood. A fireplace screen is a must.

18

THE RIGHT PRESENTATION

It is not enough to get your girlfriend a present. You have to make the extra effort so it looks, well, presentable. You can cheat and ask the store to wrap it for you, but then it will have that manufactured look. Besides, no matter what the finished product looks like, your sincere attempt to wrap the gift is more important than the appearance of the package. Follow the directions at right. And as long as you're going to all the trouble, spend money on an attractive paper of a good weight. Avoid preassembled bows. A flawed but earnest bow beats a store-bought perfect one.

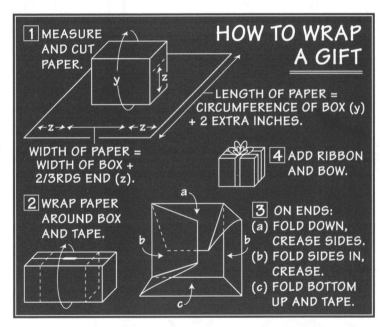

HOW TO WRAP A GIFT

1. MEASURE AND CUT PAPER.

LENGTH OF PAPER = CIRCUMFERENCE OF BOX (y) + 2 EXTRA INCHES.

WIDTH OF PAPER = WIDTH OF BOX + 2/3RDS END (z).

2. WRAP PAPER AROUND BOX AND TAPE.

3. ON ENDS:
(a) FOLD DOWN, CREASE SIDES.
(b) FOLD SIDES IN, CREASE.
(c) FOLD BOTTOM UP AND TAPE.

4. ADD RIBBON AND BOW.

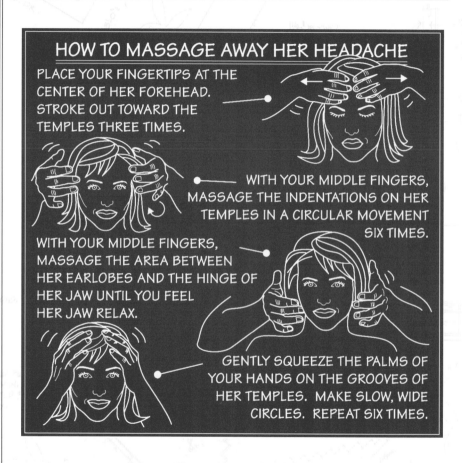

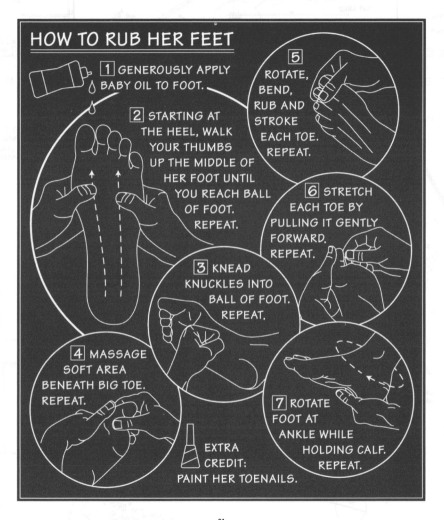

HOW TO RUB HER FEET

1. GENEROUSLY APPLY BABY OIL TO FOOT.

2. STARTING AT THE HEEL, WALK YOUR THUMBS UP THE MIDDLE OF HER FOOT UNTIL YOU REACH BALL OF FOOT. REPEAT.

3. KNEAD KNUCKLES INTO BALL OF FOOT. REPEAT.

4. MASSAGE SOFT AREA BENEATH BIG TOE. REPEAT.

5. ROTATE, BEND, RUB AND STROKE EACH TOE. REPEAT.

6. STRETCH EACH TOE BY PULLING IT GENTLY FORWARD. REPEAT.

7. ROTATE FOOT AT ANKLE WHILE HOLDING CALF. REPEAT.

EXTRA CREDIT: PAINT HER TOENAILS.

WHEN IN A CLINCH, MAKE IT A SNAP

There are enough unexpected challenges facing men these days that we should have firmly at our command those skills we know we will be called on to use. One instance where this is particularly true is when a relationship begins to flourish.

A guy needs dexterity. This is critical, especially when ushering in a new level of intimacy. Hence this blueprint. This movement should be so fluid that its gracefulness obviates any second thoughts on the woman's part. In fact, it should seem like you're doing her a favor.

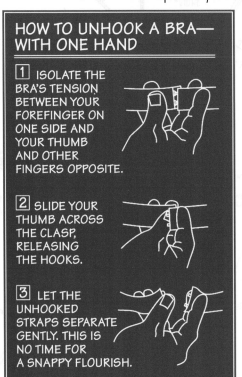

HOW TO UNHOOK A BRA—WITH ONE HAND

1. ISOLATE THE BRA'S TENSION BETWEEN YOUR FOREFINGER ON ONE SIDE AND YOUR THUMB AND OTHER FINGERS OPPOSITE.

2. SLIDE YOUR THUMB ACROSS THE CLASP, RELEASING THE HOOKS.

3. LET THE UNHOOKED STRAPS SEPARATE GENTLY. THIS IS NO TIME FOR A SNAPPY FLOURISH.

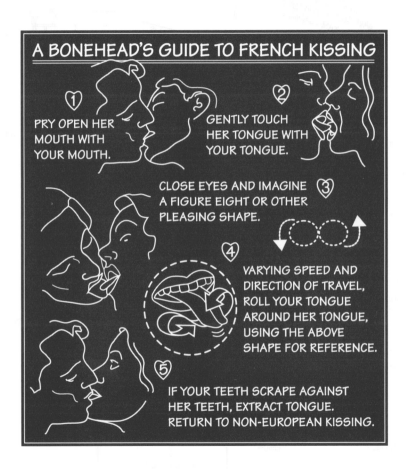

A BONEHEAD'S GUIDE TO FRENCH KISSING

① PRY OPEN HER MOUTH WITH YOUR MOUTH.

② GENTLY TOUCH HER TONGUE WITH YOUR TONGUE.

③ CLOSE EYES AND IMAGINE A FIGURE EIGHT OR OTHER PLEASING SHAPE.

④ VARYING SPEED AND DIRECTION OF TRAVEL, ROLL YOUR TONGUE AROUND HER TONGUE, USING THE ABOVE SHAPE FOR REFERENCE.

⑤ IF YOUR TEETH SCRAPE AGAINST HER TEETH, EXTRACT TONGUE. RETURN TO NON-EUROPEAN KISSING.

> "WORK IS THE CURSE
> OF THE DRINKING CLASS."
>
> — *Oscar Wilde*

DRINKING

& SMOKING

MORNING-AFTER PICK-ME-UP

If you want to make a great cappuccino, it isn't enough just to follow the instructions that come with your expensive Italian coffeemaker. You may find you're doing everything right and still getting coffee that isn't as good as what the barista at your corner coffee emporium comes up with. Instead of letting your coffeemaker be relegated, like a culinary NordicTrack, to a mere ornament

SECRETS OF A GREAT CAPPUCCINO

MILK

1 DON'T TAKE MILK OUT OF THE FRIDGE UNTIL YOU ARE READY TO FROTH IT.

2 USE METAL PITCHER FOR THE MILK.

3 POUR ONLY ABOUT AN INCH OF MILK, THEN USE A SPOON TO ADD FROTH TO THE MIXTURE.

4 DON'T KILL TASTE OF ESPRESSO WITH TOO MUCH MILK.

tucked away in a kitchen corner, follow this blueprint, and you'll foam your way to a better cup of cappuccino in no time.

MIXER ELIXIR

We found this crowd-pleasing cocktail zippy and not overly filling (as happens with some tomato juice concoctions), with just a hint of brininess. It was—as it needed to be—bracing, bold, restorative, delicious. Of course, you can vary the horseradish and hot sauce to increase the heat. The best recommendation for this recipe is that, unlike most bloody marys, you can have a second.

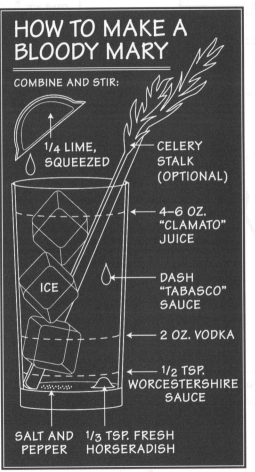

HOW TO MAKE A BLOODY MARY

COMBINE AND STIR:

1/4 LIME, SQUEEZED

CELERY STALK (OPTIONAL)

4–6 OZ. "CLAMATO" JUICE

DASH "TABASCO" SAUCE

ICE

2 OZ. VODKA

1/2 TSP. WORCESTERSHIRE SAUCE

SALT AND PEPPER

1/3 TSP. FRESH HORSERADISH

HOW TO MAKE A DAIQUIRI

SUGAR

1/2 OZ. LIME JUICE

11/2 OZ. LIGHT RUM

HOW TO MAKE A SCREWDRIVER

4 OZ. ORANGE JUICE

11/2 OZ. VODKA

HOW TO MAKE A WHISKEY SOUR

SUGAR → * * * * *

1 OZ. → LEMON JUICE

1 1/2 OZ. → WHISKEY

HOW TO MAKE A MARGARITA

SALT RIM → + + +

1/2 OZ. TRIPLE SEC →

3/4 OZ. LIME JUICE →

1 1/2 OZ. TEQUILA →

GOOD HEAD

Give Thomas Hutschenreuter two bottles from the same case of beer, and he can tell which was near the hand hole (exposure to light can skunk it ever so slightly). As master brewer for Beck's, he takes his beer seriously. As this blueprint shows, he is particular about pouring. Our advice: Repeat the exercise until you get it right.

HOW TO POUR A BEER

MAKE THREE POURS:

1 POUR OUT HALF OF BOTTLE. LET FOAM SETTLE.

BOTTLE AT 40° ANGLE

1/2 FOAM
1/2 BEER

NO TILTING!

2 POUR AGAIN. LET FOAM SETTLE.

3 POUR AGAIN. ENJOY.

BEER MUST BE 43°–46° F. FOR BEST AROMA AND HEAD.

SOAP RESIDUE ON GLASS WILL AFFECT HEAD.

HOW TO MAKE A HIGHBALL

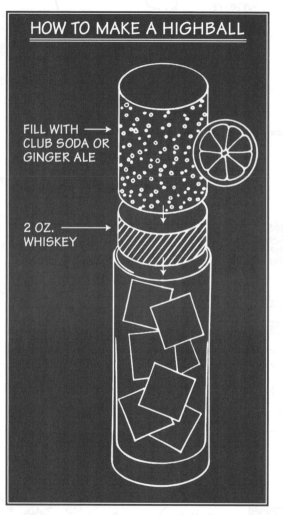

FILL WITH → CLUB SODA OR GINGER ALE

2 OZ. → WHISKEY

HOW TO MAKE A GIN AND TONIC

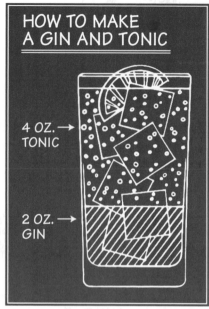

4 OZ. → TONIC

2 OZ. → GIN

THE MANHATTAN PROJECT

Named after New York's Manhattan Club, the manhattan—full-bodied and flavorful—is the perfect fall quaff after a summer of gin and tonics. Make it with two ounces of bourbon, half an ounce of sweet vermouth and a dash or two of Angostura bitters, all stirred and strained into a chilled manhattan glass. Garnish with a maraschino cherry. (A quarter ounce each of sweet and dry vermouth makes a perfect manhattan.)

HOW TO MAKE A MANHATTAN

jigger = 1 1/2 oz.

1. COMBINE:
   - 2 OUNCES OF BOURBON
   - 1/2 OUNCE SWEET VERMOUTH
   - 1 OR 2 DASHES OF ANGOSTURA BITTERS

2. STIR WITH CRACKED ICE

3. STRAIN INTO CHILLED COCKTAIL GLASS

STRAINER

4. GARNISH WITH MARASCHINO CHERRY

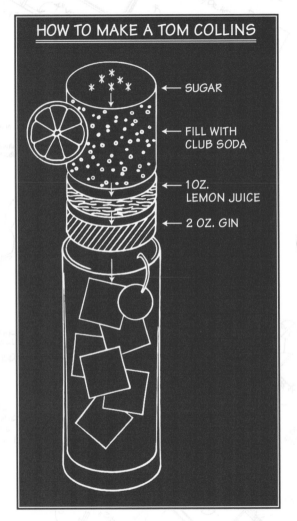

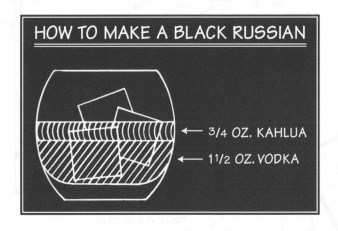

HOW TO CHILL CHAMPAGNE QUICKLY

1. FILL LARGE ICE BUCKET WITH 2/3 ICE, 1/3 WATER AND 1/2 CUP OF SALT

2. SUBMERGE BOTTLE IN BUCKET FOR 20 MINUTES

3. TO OPEN CHAMPAGNE: REMOVE WIRE, PLACE CLOTH OVER CORK; HOLD BOTTLE AT 45° ANGLE, POINT AWAY FROM YOU; TURN BOTTLE, NOT CORK.

HOW TO READ A BORDEAUX WINE LABEL

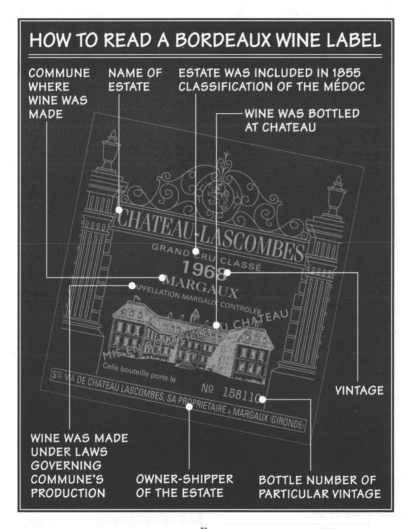

COMMUNE WHERE WINE WAS MADE

NAME OF ESTATE

ESTATE WAS INCLUDED IN 1855 CLASSIFICATION OF THE MÉDOC

WINE WAS BOTTLED AT CHATEAU

VINTAGE

WINE WAS MADE UNDER LAWS GOVERNING COMMUNE'S PRODUCTION

OWNER-SHIPPER OF THE ESTATE

BOTTLE NUMBER OF PARTICULAR VINTAGE

WINE DECANTING 101

A red wine with more than ten years of age should be decanted to remove natural sediment. We consulted Kevin Zraly's *Windows on the World Complete Wine Course* to make our blueprint. Or try pouring wine through an unbleached coffee filter. Purists may shudder, but it works.

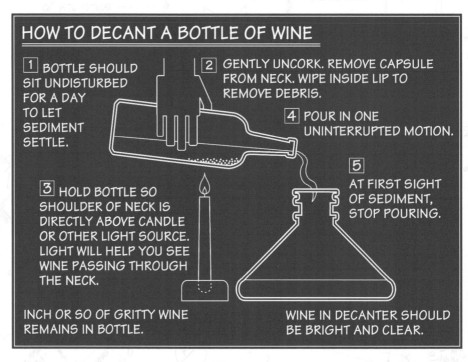

HOW TO DECANT A BOTTLE OF WINE

1. BOTTLE SHOULD SIT UNDISTURBED FOR A DAY TO LET SEDIMENT SETTLE.

2. GENTLY UNCORK. REMOVE CAPSULE FROM NECK. WIPE INSIDE LIP TO REMOVE DEBRIS.

4. POUR IN ONE UNINTERRUPTED MOTION.

3. HOLD BOTTLE SO SHOULDER OF NECK IS DIRECTLY ABOVE CANDLE OR OTHER LIGHT SOURCE. LIGHT WILL HELP YOU SEE WINE PASSING THROUGH THE NECK.

5. AT FIRST SIGHT OF SEDIMENT, STOP POURING.

INCH OR SO OF GRITTY WINE REMAINS IN BOTTLE.

WINE IN DECANTER SHOULD BE BRIGHT AND CLEAR.

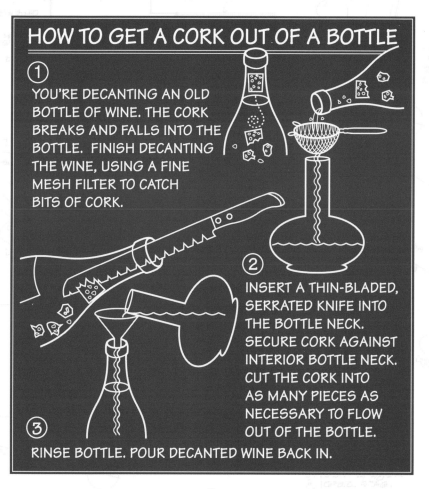

HOW TO GET A CORK OUT OF A BOTTLE

① YOU'RE DECANTING AN OLD BOTTLE OF WINE. THE CORK BREAKS AND FALLS INTO THE BOTTLE. FINISH DECANTING THE WINE, USING A FINE MESH FILTER TO CATCH BITS OF CORK.

② INSERT A THIN-BLADED, SERRATED KNIFE INTO THE BOTTLE NECK. SECURE CORK AGAINST INTERIOR BOTTLE NECK. CUT THE CORK INTO AS MANY PIECES AS NECESSARY TO FLOW OUT OF THE BOTTLE.

③ RINSE BOTTLE. POUR DECANTED WINE BACK IN.

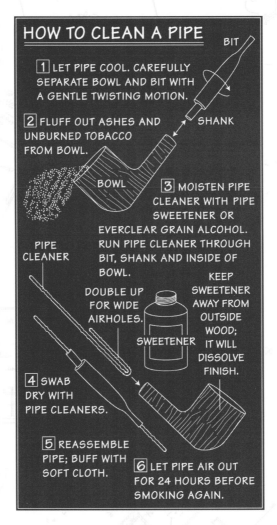

HOW TO CLEAN A PIPE

BIT

1 LET PIPE COOL. CAREFULLY SEPARATE BOWL AND BIT WITH A GENTLE TWISTING MOTION.

2 FLUFF OUT ASHES AND UNBURNED TOBACCO FROM BOWL.

SHANK

BOWL

3 MOISTEN PIPE CLEANER WITH PIPE SWEETENER OR EVERCLEAR GRAIN ALCOHOL. RUN PIPE CLEANER THROUGH BIT, SHANK AND INSIDE OF BOWL.

PIPE CLEANER

DOUBLE UP FOR WIDE AIRHOLES.

SWEETENER

KEEP SWEETENER AWAY FROM OUTSIDE WOOD; IT WILL DISSOLVE FINISH.

4 SWAB DRY WITH PIPE CLEANERS.

5 REASSEMBLE PIPE; BUFF WITH SOFT CLOTH.

6 LET PIPE AIR OUT FOR 24 HOURS BEFORE SMOKING AGAIN.

PIPE DREAMS

Is the price of premium stogies still a bit much? Lighten up—it takes less than a buck's worth of tobacco to fill a pipe, and the smoke lasts as long as a double corona. First, make sure your tobacco is properly humidified—70 percent is ideal. (It should feel slightly moist.) Fill the bowl with tobacco. Tap the side of the bowl to settle the tobacco, then gently tamp the tobacco down so it feels springy. Repeat this process two more times until the bowl is filled to the top. It takes two matches to light a pipe. First is the "false light." While puffing slowly, walk the flame over the entire surface of the tobacco, charring it evenly. Then tamp gently. This creates a cap that ensures an even light with the second match.

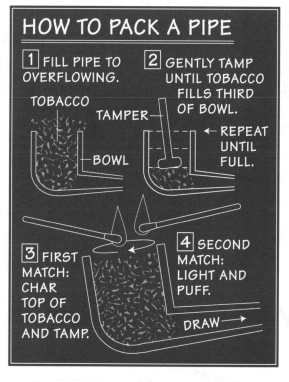

HOW TO PACK A PIPE

1 FILL PIPE TO OVERFLOWING.

TOBACCO

BOWL

2 GENTLY TAMP UNTIL TOBACCO FILLS THIRD OF BOWL.

TAMPER

← REPEAT UNTIL FULL.

3 FIRST MATCH: CHAR TOP OF TOBACCO AND TAMP.

4 SECOND MATCH: LIGHT AND PUFF.

DRAW →

> "THERE'S NOTHING LIKE GOOD FOOD, GOOD WINE AND A BAD GIRL."
>
> — fortune cookie

Eating
&
Entertaining

ART OF THE SHELL

Dismantling and eating a boiled lobster is one of the great joys of seafood.
Use the easy-to-follow blueprint at right to get the most out of the experience.

There are crustacean fanatics who suck the meat from the legs and savor the green tomalley. But if you're that hungry, just order another lobster.

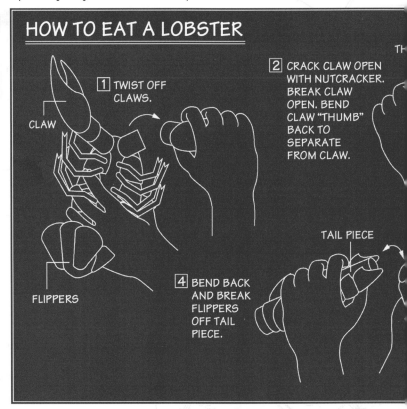

HOW TO EAT A LOBSTER

1 TWIST OFF CLAWS.

CLAW

2 CRACK CLAW OPEN WITH NUTCRACKER. BREAK CLAW OPEN. BEND CLAW "THUMB" BACK TO SEPARATE FROM CLAW.

TH

TAIL PIECE

4 BEND BACK AND BREAK FLIPPERS OFF TAIL PIECE.

FLIPPERS

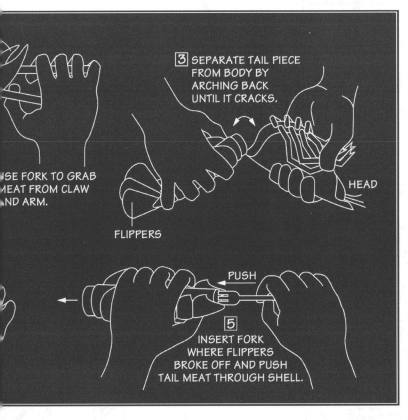

SE FORK TO GRAB MEAT FROM CLAW AND ARM.

③ SEPARATE TAIL PIECE FROM BODY BY ARCHING BACK UNTIL IT CRACKS.

HEAD

FLIPPERS

PUSH

⑤ INSERT FORK WHERE FLIPPERS BROKE OFF AND PUSH TAIL MEAT THROUGH SHELL.

A Hearty Beach Party

New Englanders figured out a long time ago that a clambake is the best way to entertain a large group of people on the beach. Dig a pit and line it with stones, light a fire in the pit and let it burn down to the coals. Assemble the ingredients according to the blueprint below and let steam for up to 90 minutes. If you want to create a clambake in the city, use a steel washtub.

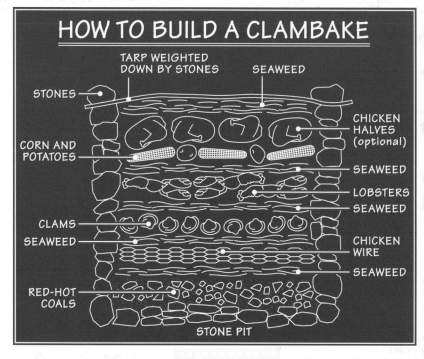

HOW TO BUILD A CLAMBAKE

TARP WEIGHTED DOWN BY STONES

SEAWEED

STONES

CHICKEN HALVES (optional)

CORN AND POTATOES

SEAWEED

LOBSTERS

SEAWEED

CLAMS

SEAWEED

CHICKEN WIRE

SEAWEED

RED-HOT COALS

STONE PIT

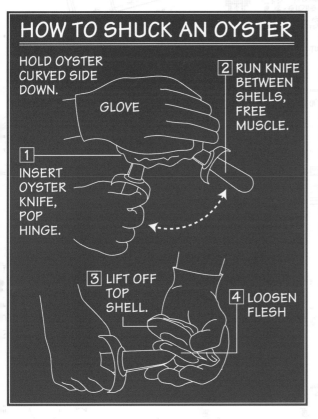

HOW TO SHUCK AN OYSTER

HOLD OYSTER CURVED SIDE DOWN.

GLOVE

2 RUN KNIFE BETWEEN SHELLS, FREE MUSCLE.

1 INSERT OYSTER KNIFE, POP HINGE.

3 LIFT OFF TOP SHELL.

4 LOOSEN FLESH

Opening an oyster shouldn't be such a struggle that it prevents you from enjoying this culinary treat. Using a stout oyster knife, find the weak point in the hinge and wiggle in the blade to release it. The rest is fairly easy if you use the blueprint at the left. Usually there is a muscle at the two o'clock position (when the hinge is facing you) that you try to free after you've loosened the hinge. It's a good idea to wear a mail glove to prevent injury if the knife slips.

Two Billion People Can't Be Wrong

Much of the world already knows how to use chopsticks, but that skill has not caught on much here in the U.S. Use the blueprint at right to learn how. Practice enough and things will just click. As you become proficient with chopsticks, you'll find some foods actually become easier to eat: noodles, for instance. Incidentally, we are seeing a boom in high-end chopsticks. At the top end, luxury chopsticks in ebony or ivory resin are tipped with silver or Chinese lacquer.

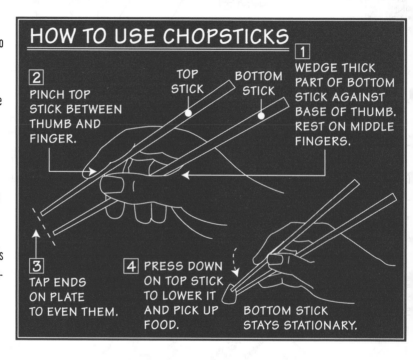

HOW TO USE CHOPSTICKS

1 WEDGE THICK PART OF BOTTOM STICK AGAINST BASE OF THUMB. REST ON MIDDLE FINGERS.

2 PINCH TOP STICK BETWEEN THUMB AND FINGER.

TOP STICK

BOTTOM STICK

3 TAP ENDS ON PLATE TO EVEN THEM.

4 PRESS DOWN ON TOP STICK TO LOWER IT AND PICK UP FOOD.

BOTTOM STICK STAYS STATIONARY.

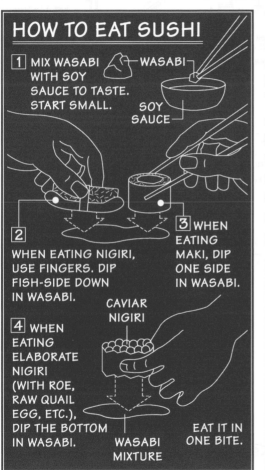

HOW TO EAT SUSHI

1. MIX WASABI WITH SOY SAUCE TO TASTE. START SMALL.

WASABI

SOY SAUCE

2. WHEN EATING NIGIRI, USE FINGERS. DIP FISH-SIDE DOWN IN WASABI.

3. WHEN EATING MAKI, DIP ONE SIDE IN WASABI.

CAVIAR NIGIRI

4. WHEN EATING ELABORATE NIGIRI (WITH ROE, RAW QUAIL EGG, ETC.), DIP THE BOTTOM IN WASABI.

WASABI MIXTURE

EAT IT IN ONE BITE.

RAW COURAGE

Using the blueprint at left, you can get the basics of eating sushi. But there are other things you should know: First, never order a drink from the sushi chef. That's what your waiter is for. It's perfectly fine — a good idea, even — to buy your chef a drink. Have the waiter ask him what he wants. It's improper, by the way, to return a half-eaten nigiri to your plate. Hold it until you finish it. If you're feeling adventurous, let the chef serve you. He will pick out what fish is best and lead you through a succession of pieces in their proper order.

Be Sharp

It's impressive the way chefs get down to business by moving their knives against an upraised steel. And this blurred activity, when done properly, trues the edge and makes the knife better to work with. There are those who insist that the only way to significantly improve a knife's cutting ability is to sharpen it on a stone, but we'll let that argument pass. In the meantime, the blueprint at left shows you how to master the art of being a hone boy.

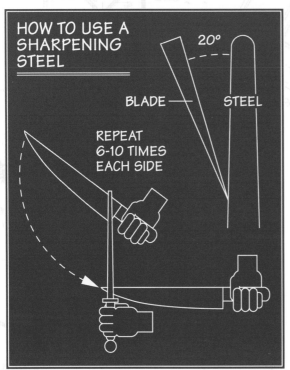

HOW TO USE A SHARPENING STEEL

20°

BLADE — STEEL

REPEAT 6-10 TIMES EACH SIDE

TALKING TURKEY

The table is set and appetites are whetted. It's your job to carve the bird without making it look like roadkill. Here's how: Use a steel to make sure your carving knife is sharp. Insert a carving fork where the thighbone meets the body. Separate the joint and bend the leg and thigh downward. (You can also separate the leg from the thigh if you like.) Carve the meat off the bone in quarter-inch slices. Arrange the meat on a heated platter. That takes care of the dark meat. Next, begin halfway up the breast and use a steady stroke to cut thin and even slices to the bone. (Switch to a long, serrated knife for smoother cut. If you remove the wishbone, carving the breast will be easy.) Continue slicing, starting at a higher point each time until the crest of the bone is reached. If you need more meat, go ahead and carve the other side. Don't forget the stuffing, but don't sweat the little stuff. It's more important to eat it while it's hot.

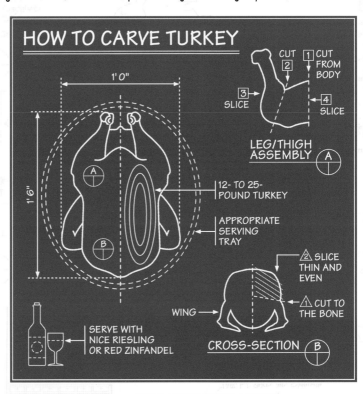

HOW TO CARVE TURKEY

1' 0"
1' 6"

CUT 2
1 CUT FROM BODY
3 SLICE
4 SLICE

LEG/THIGH ASSEMBLY (A)

12- TO 25- POUND TURKEY

APPROPRIATE SERVING TRAY

2 SLICE THIN AND EVEN

WING
1 CUT TO THE BONE

CROSS-SECTION (B)

SERVE WITH NICE RIESLING OR RED ZINFANDEL

WELL DONE

When you grill a steak, you need to master the art of knowing when it's done. Amateurs cut open the steak and check the color. This drains the beef of its juices and dries it out. The best way to tell when it's done is to acquire a feel for the changing consistency of the meat. Use the blueprint at left. As always, let the meat rest a few minutes before you slice it.

HOW TO CHECK A STEAK

RARE

MEDIUM

WELL DONE

ATTENTION, CARNIVORES

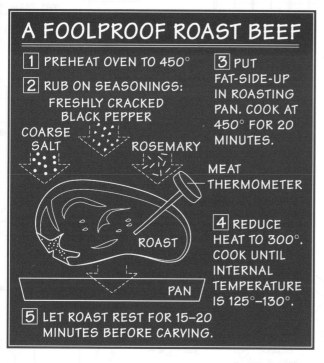

A FOOLPROOF ROAST BEEF

1. PREHEAT OVEN TO 450°

2. RUB ON SEASONINGS:
   FRESHLY CRACKED
   BLACK PEPPER
   COARSE
   SALT
   ROSEMARY

3. PUT FAT-SIDE-UP IN ROASTING PAN. COOK AT 450° FOR 20 MINUTES.

MEAT THERMOMETER

ROAST

PAN

4. REDUCE HEAT TO 300°. COOK UNTIL INTERNAL TEMPERATURE IS 125°–130°.

5. LET ROAST REST FOR 15–20 MINUTES BEFORE CARVING.

The traditional dinner mainstay is remarkably easy to prepare. Start with an eight–ten pound standing rib roast — with rib bones attached. Take it out of the refrigerator and let it come to room temperature — 30–40 minutes. Follow the blueprint at left. Place the roast in a pan outfitted with a rack, so the juices can run off. Insert a needle-nose meat thermometer in the thickest part of the roast and away from any bones for an accurate reading to determine doneness.

> ### "SPORTS DO NOT BUILD CHARACTER. THEY REVEAL IT."
>
> — Heywood Broun

SPORT

&

SURVIVAL

Brim Shot

You've got yourself a new baseball cap, but you want it to look well-seasoned instead of like rookie headgear just out of the box. First, do as the blueprint at right says and cut out the mesh liner behind the front brim. Your cap fits better already. Then bend the brim around your fist to get a good curve and fold it through the hole that the strap makes in the back. Now run the cap through the washing machine a couple of times, stamp it into the dirt and throw it at a tree. Now it's looking good.

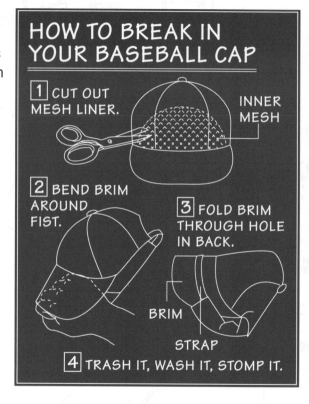

HOW TO BREAK IN YOUR BASEBALL CAP

1 CUT OUT MESH LINER.

INNER MESH

2 BEND BRIM AROUND FIST.

3 FOLD BRIM THROUGH HOLE IN BACK.

BRIM

STRAP

4 TRASH IT, WASH IT, STOMP IT.

LOVE YOUR GLOVE

When leaves turn to green, a young man's fancy turns to baseball. If you've been out of the ballpark for a while and buy a new glove, you'll need to spend time breaking it in. This is a satisfying ritual that will remind you of your boyhood. Anything leather gets better with use. In time a leather mitt will conform to your hand, making it easier to catch a ball, fish it out and throw it. Follow the blueprint here. Use a high-quality leather oil and work it into the palm of the glove before you form it around the ball and secure it with rubber bands. Putting it under your mattress is optional. Be sure to interrupt this process and use the glove for pickup games. The more you play with it, oil it and flex it, the more pliant it will become.

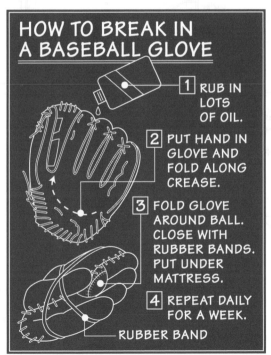

HOW TO BREAK IN A BASEBALL GLOVE

1. RUB IN LOTS OF OIL.

2. PUT HAND IN GLOVE AND FOLD ALONG CREASE.

3. FOLD GLOVE AROUND BALL. CLOSE WITH RUBBER BANDS. PUT UNDER MATTRESS.

4. REPEAT DAILY FOR A WEEK.

RUBBER BAND

KICK BACK

Don't expect your Tae-Bo training to prepare you for the advanced legwork of the roundhouse kick. The circular, sweeping motion of this martial arts technique is ideal for disarming thugs, and it can create an opening for a pulverizing punch. But its legwork requires practice — first in front of a mirror and then with a sparring partner. Tip: You can use the roundhouse as a "jab" to intimidate an attacker. If you're lucky, he'll mistake you for Jackie Chan and split.

HOW TO DO A ROUNDHOUSE KICK

1 STAND AT 90° ANGLE TO TARGET.

2 PIVOT ON BALL OF LEAD FOOT, TURNING HEEL 90° TOWARD TARGET.

3 ROLL HIP FORWARD.

4 LIFT KNEE UP AND OUT.

5 KEEP LOWER LEG HORIZONTAL AND COCKED HIGH.

6 SNAP OUT LEG IN CIRCULAR MOTION, STRIKE WITH TOP OF FOOT.

7 RECOCK LEG AND ROTATE BACK TO FIRST POSITION.

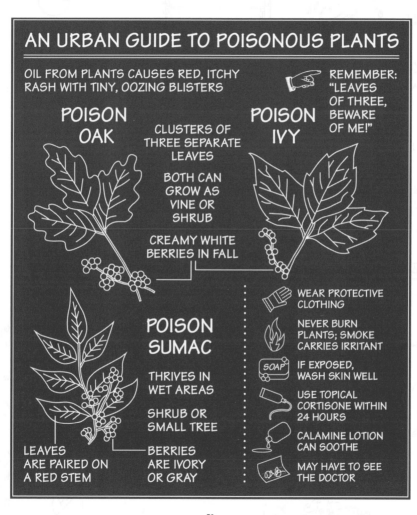

AN URBAN GUIDE TO POISONOUS PLANTS

OIL FROM PLANTS CAUSES RED, ITCHY
RASH WITH TINY, OOZING BLISTERS

REMEMBER:
"LEAVES
OF THREE,
BEWARE
OF ME!"

POISON OAK

POISON IVY

CLUSTERS OF
THREE SEPARATE
LEAVES

BOTH CAN
GROW AS
VINE OR
SHRUB

CREAMY WHITE
BERRIES IN FALL

POISON SUMAC

THRIVES IN
WET AREAS

SHRUB OR
SMALL TREE

LEAVES
ARE PAIRED ON
A RED STEM

BERRIES
ARE IVORY
OR GRAY

WEAR PROTECTIVE
CLOTHING

NEVER BURN
PLANTS; SMOKE
CARRIES IRRITANT

IF EXPOSED,
WASH SKIN WELL

USE TOPICAL
CORTISONE WITHIN
24 HOURS

CALAMINE LOTION
CAN SOOTHE

MAY HAVE TO SEE
THE DOCTOR

SLIPPERY WHEN WET

So you've finally caught the big one and you are not going to throw it back nor even hang it on the wall. This one you're going to eat. A noble fish shouldn't be mangled by amateur handling after the catch. Follow the directions in the blueprint at right and you'll have a pair of clean fillets to broil, sauté or bake. A cautionary note: Always move the knife blade away from you. Fish are dangerously slippery.

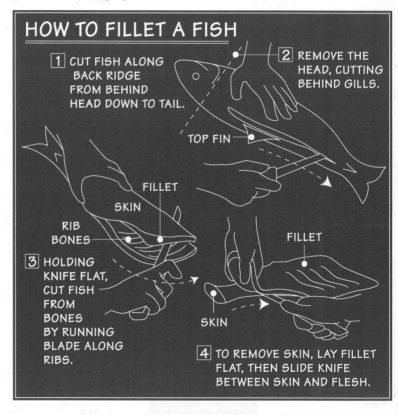

HOW TO FILLET A FISH

1 CUT FISH ALONG BACK RIDGE FROM BEHIND HEAD DOWN TO TAIL.

2 REMOVE THE HEAD, CUTTING BEHIND GILLS.

TOP FIN

FILLET

SKIN

RIB BONES

FILLET

3 HOLDING KNIFE FLAT, CUT FISH FROM BONES BY RUNNING BLADE ALONG RIBS.

SKIN

4 TO REMOVE SKIN, LAY FILLET FLAT, THEN SLIDE KNIFE BETWEEN SKIN AND FLESH.

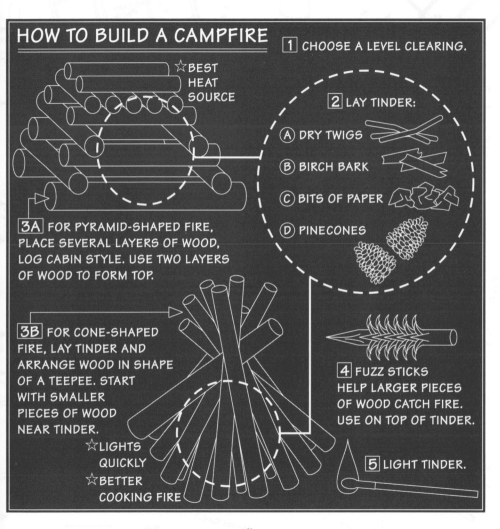

HOW TO BUILD A CAMPFIRE

1 CHOOSE A LEVEL CLEARING.

☆ BEST HEAT SOURCE

2 LAY TINDER:

Ⓐ DRY TWIGS

Ⓑ BIRCH BARK

Ⓒ BITS OF PAPER

Ⓓ PINECONES

3A FOR PYRAMID-SHAPED FIRE, PLACE SEVERAL LAYERS OF WOOD, LOG CABIN STYLE. USE TWO LAYERS OF WOOD TO FORM TOP.

3B FOR CONE-SHAPED FIRE, LAY TINDER AND ARRANGE WOOD IN SHAPE OF A TEEPEE. START WITH SMALLER PIECES OF WOOD NEAR TINDER.

☆ LIGHTS QUICKLY
☆ BETTER COOKING FIRE

4 FUZZ STICKS HELP LARGER PIECES OF WOOD CATCH FIRE. USE ON TOP OF TINDER.

5 LIGHT TINDER.

"LIFE CONSISTS NOT IN
HOLDING GOOD CARDS
BUT IN PLAYING THOSE
YOU HOLD WELL."

— Josh Billings

CARDS

&

DICE

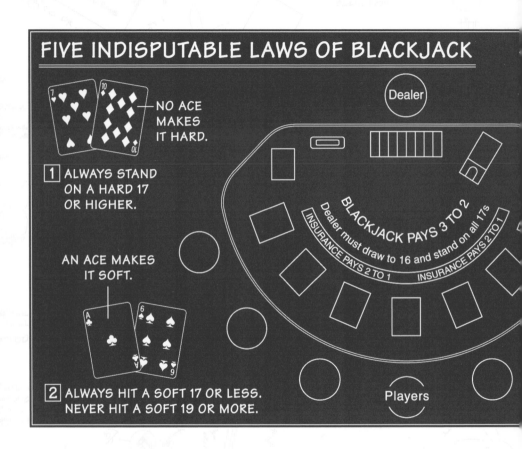

FIVE INDISPUTABLE LAWS OF BLACKJACK

NO ACE MAKES IT HARD.

1 ALWAYS STAND ON A HARD 17 OR HIGHER.

AN ACE MAKES IT SOFT.

2 ALWAYS HIT A SOFT 17 OR LESS. NEVER HIT A SOFT 19 OR MORE.

Dealer

BLACKJACK PAYS 3 TO 2
Dealer must draw to 16 and stand on all 17s
INSURANCE PAYS 2 TO 1   INSURANCE PAYS 2 TO 1

Players

Hit Me

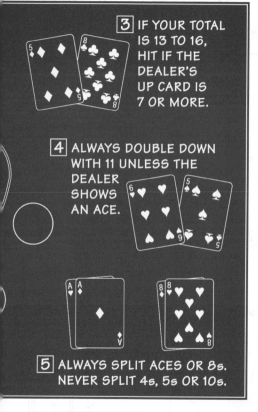

3 IF YOUR TOTAL IS 13 TO 16, HIT IF THE DEALER'S UP CARD IS 7 OR MORE.

4 ALWAYS DOUBLE DOWN WITH 11 UNLESS THE DEALER SHOWS AN ACE.

5 ALWAYS SPLIT ACES OR 8s. NEVER SPLIT 4s, 5s OR 10s.

Blackjack, or 21, is the most popular casino game. It's simple and, if played correctly, gives the casino only a slight advantage. While skilled card counters can beat the house, the rest of us have to rely on knowing which combination of cards to hit on and which to stand on. With this knowledge, you'll be able to play the casino close to even. Remember, your goal is to beat the dealer, not just to get as close to 21 as possible. At left are five indisputable rules to follow when you're playing the type of six- or eight-deck blackjack most commonly dealt in Las Vegas. (These rules don't apply in casinos where single-deck blackjack is dealt.)

THE BEST BEGINNER'S BETS AT CRAPS

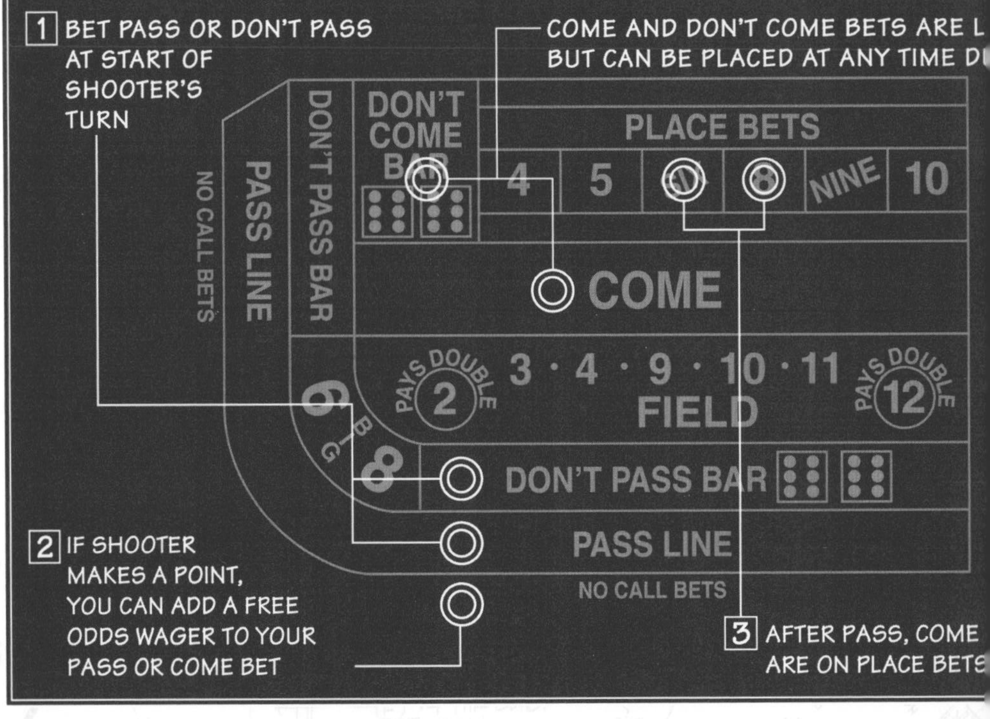

1 BET PASS OR DON'T PASS AT START OF SHOOTER'S TURN

COME AND DON'T COME BETS ARE L
BUT CAN BE PLACED AT ANY TIME DU

NO CALL BETS

PASS LINE

DON'T PASS BAR

DON'T COME BAR

PLACE BETS

4 5 ⊙ ⊙ NINE 10

⊙ COME

PAYS DOUBLE (2) 3 · 4 · 9 · 10 · 11 FIELD PAYS DOUBLE (12)

6 B G 8

⊙ DON'T PASS BAR

⊙ PASS LINE

NO CALL BETS

⊙

2 IF SHOOTER MAKES A POINT, YOU CAN ADD A FREE ODDS WAGER TO YOUR PASS OR COME BET

3 AFTER PASS, COME ARE ON PLACE BETS

TUMBLIN' DICE

Step into any casino and follow the cheers. Odds are good you'll end up at a craps table. That's because craps is a game that offers some of the best odds in a casino. But it's also one of the most intimidating. Here's how to join the action. [1] Betting Pass or Don't Pass at the start of a shooter's turn means you're betting the shooter wins (Pass) or loses (Don't Pass) on the first roll. Either bet pays even money. Betting Come or Don't Come has the same payback, but these bets are placed any time after the shooter's first roll. [2] If the shooter makes a point (i.e., rolls a four, five, six, eight, nine or ten— announced by the stickman), you can add a Free Odds wager, basically increasing your original Pass or Come bets. This is a great bet, with no house edge. If the shooter then rolls that point before rolling a seven, the bet pays off at the true odds: six to five for a six or an eight, three to two for a five or a nine, and two to one for a four or a ten. [3] After a Pass, Come or Free Odds bet, the best place to put your money is on a Place bet on the six or the eight. Either pays seven to six if the shooter rolls your number before a seven.

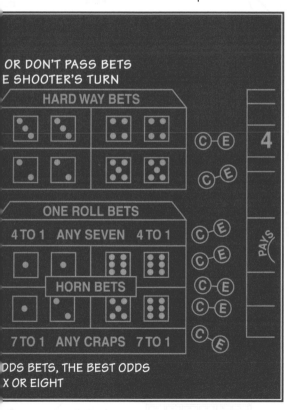

OR DON'T PASS BETS
E SHOOTER'S TURN

HARD WAY BETS

ONE ROLL BETS

4 TO 1   ANY SEVEN   4 TO 1

HORN BETS

7 TO 1   ANY CRAPS   7 TO 1

DDS BETS, THE BEST ODDS
X OR EIGHT

SLOTS SMARTS

No casino game offers so much for so little as slots. To increase your chances: (1) Join the slot club. It's free and you get a rebate of up to one percent on bets, plus complimentary or discounted meals and rooms. (2) Play in casinos. Avoid airports, restaurants or supermarkets, where odds are worse. In Nevada, slots can pay back as little as 75 percent, but most casinos offer more than 90 percent as an inducement. (3) The higher the jackpot the worse the odds: Machines with lower jackpots pay out smaller wins more frequently, so if you're not going for the big payday, play these. (4) On all progressive and most other slots, play the maximum number of coins. If your budget is tight, choose a cheaper slot. (5) Play the highest-denomination machine you can. The house edge decreases as the price rises.

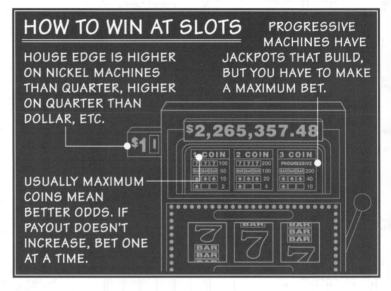

HOW TO WIN AT SLOTS

HOUSE EDGE IS HIGHER ON NICKEL MACHINES THAN QUARTER, HIGHER ON QUARTER THAN DOLLAR, ETC.

PROGRESSIVE MACHINES HAVE JACKPOTS THAT BUILD, BUT YOU HAVE TO MAKE A MAXIMUM BET.

USUALLY MAXIMUM COINS MEAN BETTER ODDS. IF PAYOUT DOESN'T INCREASE, BET ONE AT A TIME.

$2,265,357.48

1 COIN	2 COIN	3 COIN
7 7 7 100	7 7 7 200	PROGRESSIVE
BAR BAR BAR 50	BAR BAR BAR 100	BAR BAR BAR 200
10	20	40
2	4	10

Don't Lose the Winnings

Last but not least, here's how to stash your cash (or cache your stash, as the case may be). This blueprint shows some sure-fire ways to keep secret items secreted away. Even James Bond couldn't come up with a better place to hide his goodies.

HOW TO MAKE A SECRET HIDING PLACE

COAT RACK CONCEALER
CUT OUT WALL BEHIND COAT HOOK.

STRAP VALUABLES TO WALL STUD OR USE SPRING CLIP.

SHOWER ROD STASH

PLACE IN PLASTIC BAG AND ATTACH STRING FOR EASY REMOVAL.

UNDER-STAIR CLOSET

STAIR SAFE
CONCEAL HINGES ON INSIDE OF STAIR RISER OR FALSE WALL.

FALSE WALL

INDEX

"You only live once,
and the way I live, once is enough."
— Frank Sinatra